death and resurrection of Jesus

Julie Moser

10 Publishing
a division of 10 of those.com

Published in 2013 by 10Publishing, a division of 10ofthose.com

9D Centurion Court, Farington, Leyland PR25 3UQ, England.

Email: info@10ofthose.com Website: www.10ofthose.com

ISBN 978-1-909611-35-1

Printed in the UK

death and resurrection of Jesus

contents

leader's notes available through
www.effectiveyouthministry.com

death and resurrection of Jesus
introduction

Welcome to Death and Resurrection of Jesus!

These studies are designed to help you understand the most important event in history – the death and resurrection of Jesus.

Jesus was a great teacher, healer, miracle worker and friend of sinners. However, he was not popular with everyone who met him. The religious leaders of his day were jealous and threatened by his popularity and message. They organized his arrest and had him sentenced to death by crucifixion on a cross. However, the story does not end here. Three days later he rose from the dead and appeared to his disciples and many others.

Luke walks us through the last days and hours of Jesus' life. As we study this important event in history, we will come to see how it has big consequences for us today.

Julie Moser

Death and Resurrection of Jesus

The Last Supper

Luke 22:7-23

"For you know that it was not with perishable things such as silver or gold that you were redeemed from the empty way of life handed down to you from your forefathers, but with the precious blood of Christ, a lamb without blemish or defect." 1 Peter 1:18-19

let's get started

let's get started

1 What is your favorite meal (describe every item on your plate)?

2 What do you know about the death and resurrection of Jesus?
(✔ Check from the list below what you think the correct facts are.)

- ○ Jesus died on a Friday
- ○ Jesus was crucified on a cross
- ○ Jesus was tortured
- ○ Jesus had a fair trial
- ○ Christmas celebrates his death
- ○ Jesus was betrayed
- ○ Jesus forgave the people who killed him
- ○ Jesus came to teach us to be nice people
- ○ Jesus arose on a Sunday
- ○ Jesus' body secretly disappeared

(Answers on page 42)

going deeper

going deeper

» **The Last Supper.** **Read Luke 22:7-23.**

+ How does Jesus show that he is aware of what will soon take place? (vv. 15-16, 21-22)

The Lord's Supper (vv. 17-22) is still celebrated today by Christians in remembrance of Jesus' death.

- What are we to remember when we celebrate this event?

We eat the bread to remember… (see v. 19)

We drink the wine to remember… (see v. 20)

- Why do you think it is important to regularly remember Jesus' sacrifice?

FYI **Did you know…** The Passover was an annual meal celebrated by the nation of Israel. It celebrated the night that the angel of the Lord "passed over" the homes of the Israelites to carry out the last plague on Egypt (the death of the firstborn). See Exodus 12:1-30. The blood of a lamb without defect was to be painted on the houses as a sign to the angel of death to pass over that home. Later in 1 Corinthians 5:7 Jesus is described as the Passover lamb that was sacrificed for us.

The New Covenant.

Look again at Luke 22:20

- A Covenant is an agreement between two parties binding them to be committed to each other. Another word for Covenant is "promise". Can you think of any examples of a covenant today?

God had made covenants with people in the past.
The major ones are: Noah (Gen 9:1-17), Abraham (Gen 15 and 17), Moses (Ex 19, 24 and 34) and King David (2 Sam 7:1-17, 23:5).

The New Covenant that Jesus spoke about at the last supper was the final and perfect one prophesied centuries earlier. **Read Jeremiah 31:31-34.**

- Why didn't the old covenants work according to Jeremiah?

- How is the new Covenant with Jesus different from the old ones

Brought near to God. Read Ephesians 2:11-13.

FYI

The meanings of two important words:

❶ A "Gentile" is someone who is not Jewish. ❷ "Circumcision" of a Jewish male was a sign of membership of the people of God to the covenant.

Underline the words that describe what the Gentile's relationship to God and Christ used to be in the passage below

[11]Therefore, remember that formerly you who are Gentiles by birth and called
"uncircumcised" by those who call themselves "the circumcision" (that done in the body
by the hands of men)— [12]remember that at that time you were separate from Christ,
excluded from citizenship in Israel and foreigners to the covenants of the promise,
without hope and without God in the world. [13]But now in Christ Jesus you who once
were far away have been brought near through the blood of Christ.

- What does Jesus' death do for us? (v. 13)

- What does this say to the Christian person who feels far away from God?

getting active

Helping each other

- How does the death of Jesus prove God's love for us?

- How can we help each other to remember what Jesus has done for us?

- How can we help each other when we feel that our past sin hinders our friendship with God?

let's pray

- Give thanks to God that he sent Jesus to bring us into relationship with him.
- Ask God to help you understand the importance of Jesus' death and resurrection as we look at Luke over the coming weeks.
- Share any other matters for prayer and then pray together.

stay tuned

Next week, we will look at the beginning of the fulfillment of the God's plan with the arrest of Jesus.

For your eyes only:
The week ahead

For your eyes only:
The Week ahead

1. Personal Bible Reading

This week you will look at the covenants throughout the Bible mentioned in the study. They are promises that God made to individuals throughout the Old Testament preparing the way for the final and perfect covenant made with us through the death of Jesus.

My weekly Bible reading plan!

This week, I read about the covenant with... (place a ✔ when you have read it.)

1. ☐ **Noah:** Genesis 9:1-17
2. ☐ **Abraham:** Genesis 15 and 17
3. ☐ **Moses:** Exodus 19-20
4. ☐ **King David:** 2 Samuel 7:1-17, 23:5
5. ☐ **Jesus:** Hebrews 8

Also find some time to read the passage not covered in the studies: Luke 22:24-38

2. Memory Verse

Can you learn the memory verse at the top of this study (1 Peter 1:18-19)? Give it a try this week.

For you know that it was not with perishable things such as silver or gold that you were redeemed from the empty way of life handed down to you from your forefathers, but with the precious blood of Christ, a lamb without blemish or defect.

1 Peter 1:18-19

Pray that you will continue to discover how much God loves you. Pray that you will experience freedom from guilt of past sins.

Things that I can thank God for: ____________________

____

Things that I need to pray for: ____________________

____

Understanding the Lord's Supper

The Lord's Supper or Holy Communion is a time when God's people remember the death and sacrifice of Jesus for our sin. It is traditionally done with a piece of bread and wine. When you are a regular member of a church it is important that you understand what it means to participate in this occasion. Here are some helpful tips:

1. Taking the bread and wine (or non-alcoholic grape juice in many cases) does not take away your sin or make you more holy. It is the death of Jesus that takes away your sin and makes you righteous (righteous means 'innocent'). At the Lord's Supper you remember what Jesus has done for you. It's helpful to think of the Lord's Supper as a celebration of forgiveness that is already ours.
2. Different churches have different traditions in the way they celebrate the Lord's Supper. For example: some only allow people to participate after they've been accepted into the church through a course such as confirmation; some only allow people who are baptized; some require parental approval if people are under age; some use one cup while some use individual cups for the wine/juice; some versions of communion are long and formal and some are short and casual etc. There is no one way that is the perfect, right way. You need to understand the traditions of your church and obey the format they prefer. If you attend another church as a visitor it is okay for you to celebrate the Lord's Supper with them as long as you follow their requirements.
3. Participating in the Lord's Supper recognizes relationship with Jesus as well as relationship with each other. Therefore, if you are not in a relationship with Jesus, the Lord's Supper is not for you. Likewise, if you are out of relationship with others in your church, the Bible urges you to sort out your differences before taking the Lord's Supper together (see 1 Corinthians 11:17-34).
4. The Lord's Supper is a time of joy and celebration. So an appropriate response is one of thankfulness and joy. Furthermore, it points to the great future banquet that we will celebrate together in the presence of Jesus (Luke 22:16 and Rev 19:9).

death and resurrection of Jesus

The garden of gethsemane

Luke 22:39-62

For just as through the disobedience of the one man the many were made sinners, so also through the obedience of the one man the many will be made righteous. Romans 5:19

let's get started

let's get started

1. How do you respond when your parent/s ask you to do something you don't want to do (e.g., homework, clean your room, do the dishes etc.) (Circle your answer from the options below.)

Do it right away

Complain but then do it

Pay my brother/sister to do it

Pretend to be ill or injured

Complain

Hide

Think of an excuse to not do it

Other? ___________________

2. Have you ever had to do something you really didn't want to do? What was it?

going deeper

going deeper

» **Praying in Gethsemane.** **Read Luke 22:39-46.**

+ Jesus knew he was about to be arrested and killed. What did he pray for? (v. 42)

- How is this an example for us of how to pray?

- How would you describe this time for Jesus in light of verse 44?

- Why do you think Jesus was so disappointed when the disciples fell asleep?

- How does this section prepare us for the death of Jesus? (What does it tell us about what Jesus is about to go through?)

The arrest of Jesus. **Read Luke 22:47-54.**

- Why do you think they arrested Jesus in the middle of the night?

- How did Jesus' disciples respond to his arrest? (vv. 49-50)

- How did Jesus react to their actions? (v. 51) Why do you think he reacted this way?

Peter's denial. **Read Luke 22:31-34 and 55-62.**

- Why did Peter deny knowing Jesus (his best friend) - what was he so worried about?

- Have you ever been in the same situation as Peter and denied being a follower of Jesus? What was the situation?

- Where is it hard to stand up for knowing Jesus and where is it easy?

(✔ Check the boxes and then discuss your answers.)

	Really easy	Sometimes difficult	Really hard
At home	☐	☐	☐
With relatives	☐	☐	☐
At school	☐	☐	☐
At parties	☐	☐	☐
Other place? ____________	☐	☐	☐

+ What will help you to be strong when you are tempted to be ashamed of Jesus?

+ What can you do when you are faced with a situation that tempts you to be ashamed of Jesus?

FYI Did YOU KNOW... Peter had a history of failing Jesus and getting it wrong (e.g., Matthew 14:27-31; 16:21-23; Mark 14:37; Luke 9:28-33; John 18:10-11). Although Peter failed Jesus many times and finally denied him, Jesus restored him after the resurrection (John 21:15-19).

Note: Luke 9:23-27 talks about being ashamed of Jesus. This is not talking about a one-time mistake like Peter's mistake, but a continual and permanent denial of him. The example of Peter is great news for all of us who have denied knowing Jesus in a time of weakness and fear.

Read 1 Peter 4:12-16 and see how Peter's whole attitude changed after the resurrection.

getting active

getting active

Helping each other

+ How can we help each other when we feel afraid to acknowledge that we follow Jesus?

+ How can we build each other up to be confident and courageous about our faith?

let's pray

- Thank Jesus for his obedience, even when it meant suffering and death for our sake.
- Pray that you will not be ashamed to be a follower of Jesus.
- Share any other matters for prayer and then pray together.

stay tuned Next week, we will look at the trial of Jesus.

For your eyes only:
The week ahead

For your eyes only:
The Week ahead

1. Personal Bible Reading

This week, we will read one of the books Peter wrote after Jesus died and rose again. As you read it keep in mind how Peter struggled with standing up for Jesus at his arrest and trial and how later he became a bold believer.

My weekly Bible reading plan!

In the book of 1 Peter, I read.. (place a ✔ when you have read it.)

☐ Chapter 1 ☐ Chapter 2 ☐ Chapter 3 ☐ Chapter 4 ☐ Chapter 5

2. Memory Verse

Can you learn the memory verse at the top of this study (Romans 5:19)? Give it a try this week.

You may like to read the verse in context to understand what you are memorizing. Read Romans 5:12-21. This passage tells us that sin and disobedience came through one man, Adam (Genesis 3) and righteousness and obedience came through one man, Jesus (through his death and resurrection).

For just as through the disobedience of the one man the many were made sinners, so also through the obedience of the one man the many will be made righteous. Romans 5:19

Pray for courage when you face suffering or ridicule for following Jesus. Pray that you will show that you follow Jesus by the way that you live.

Things that I can thank God for: ______

______

Things that I need to pray for: ______

______

Jesus: the obedient sacrifice for our sins

The account of Jesus praying in Gethsemane shows us that Jesus willingly laid down his life for us. While it was the Father's plan and will, Jesus was not a victim but chose to obey. Read the following passages and answer the questions below:

What do these passages tell us about Jesus' death for us?

Philippians 2:5-11

John 10:11-18

Ephesians 5:1-2

1 John 3:16

Hot tips for standing up for Jesus.

1. Do your best to show that you follow Jesus by the way that you live (see 1 Timothy 4:12).
2. Be committed to regular fellowship with other believers (see Hebrews 10:24-25). Doing this helps you in your faith, helps your fellow Christians and shows everyone that following Jesus is a priority.
3. When people see that you are different because of your life, be prepared to explain why you are different (see 1 Peter 3:15-16). You might like to learn a simple explanation of what a Christian believes. Perhaps practice with your Christian friends, questioning each other about the Christian faith and answering each other's questions.

Death and Resurrection of Jesus

The Trial of Jesus

Luke 22:63~23:25

God made him who had no sin to be sin for us, so that in him we might become the righteousness of God. 2 Corinthians 5:21

let's get started

let's get started

Share What would you do if…

- you saw a helpless old woman being robbed?
- you saw someone younger than you being bullied at school?
- one of your friends had nasty or untrue things written about them on the internet?

- Is it hard to stand up for injustice?
- Have you ever been treated unfairly?

going deeper

going deeper

Jesus before the Council of elders. Read Luke 22:63-71.

- What happened to Jesus before his trial began (vv. 63-65)?

What would happen today if the law courts mistreated or tortured someone before he/she even went to trial?

What does this tell you about Jesus' trial?

What did Jesus reveal about himself in his answers to the questions by the council of elders? (vv. 67-70)

FYI: The council of elders... (the Sanhedrin) was made up of the religious leaders of Israel.

What did the council of elders agree upon as the crime of Jesus? (vv. 70-71)

Jesus before Pilate. Read Luke 23:1-7.

What were the accusations of Jesus that the elders brought before Pilate? (v. 2)

1. ______________________________
2. ______________________________
3. ______________________________

Did any of these accusations match the interrogation of Jesus in vv. 67-71?

What accusation does Jesus acknowledge to Pilate? (v. 3)

Why do you think Pilate handed Jesus over to Herod? (vv. 4, 6-7)

Jesus before Herod. Read Luke 23:8-12.

Why do you think Jesus refused to answer Herod? (See v. 8)

What do you think the elders were accusing Jesus of in v. 10?

How did Herod treat Jesus?

What can you say about Jesus' trial so far?

Jesus before Pilate (again). Read Luke 23:13-25.

What was the final verdict of Pilate and Herod? (vv. 14-15, 22)

Why do you think Pilate eventually gave in to the crowd?

What was so wrong about the release of Barabbas in place of Jesus? (What was Barabbas guilty of, v. 19?)

FYI LUKE... shows us the real injustice in the trial of Jesus. All of this was foretold by the prophet Isaiah – see what he says in Isaiah 53:7 See also 1 Peter 2:23

The release of Barabbas (v. 25) demonstrated what Jesus' death was all about – the substitution of the innocent for the guilty. **Read the following verses**. What do they tell you about what Jesus' death?

1 Peter 2:23-25 ____________________

2 Corinthians 5:21____________________

Special note: When Jesus dies he not only takes our sin onto himself, he also credits us with his righteousness.

What is unfair about the substitution of Jesus for the unrighteous?

How is the unfair treatment of Jesus great news for us? (See Romans 3:22-24)

In Luke 6:27-31 Jesus teaches us to love our enemies and when they mistreat us to "turn the other cheek". We see Jesus living out his own teaching at his trial. Give examples of times when we can we be like Jesus and obey his teaching to "turn the other cheek"?

getting active

getting active

Helping each other

How can we help each other in our response to what Jesus has done for us?

How should we treat each other, in light of the fact that Jesus freely forgave us?

let's pray

- Thank God for sending Jesus to be our substitute.
- Thank God for forgiving us.
- Share any other matters for prayer and then pray together.

stay tuned Next week, we will learn about the death of Jesus by crucifixion

For your eyes only:
The week ahead

For your eyes only:
The Week ahead

1. Personal Bible Reading

This week, we will read a section of Romans that explains the work of Jesus' death on the cross. The major theme of Romans is the substitution of Jesus (the righteous one) for us (who are sinful). This substitution is similar to the example of Barabbas, where the guilty one goes free in place of the innocent one who is punished. These chapters are long and full of big stuff so take your time and don't worry if you are not able to take it all in. If necessary, read them a couple of times.

My weekly Bible reading plan!

In the book of Romans, I read... (place a ✔ when you have read it.)

☐ Chapter 5 ☐ Chapter 6 ☐ Chapter 7 ☐ Chapter 8

Also find some time to read the passage not covered in the studies: Luke 23:26-38

Note: Simon of Cyrene gives us an image of what it means to be a disciple of Jesus. He walked behind Jesus and carried his cross.

2. Memory Verse

Can you learn the memory verse at the top of this study (2 Corinthians 5:21)? Give it a try this week!

God made him who had no sin to be sin for us, so that in him we might become the righteousness of God. 2 Corinthians 5:21

Thank God for forgiving us instead of giving us the punishment we deserve. Ask for help to live for Jesus now that you have been set free from sin.

Things that I can thank God for: ______________________

____

____

____

Things that I need to pray for: ______________________

____

____

____

Explaining what a Christian believes

The gospel is the good news about Jesus death and resurrection. Learn to explain it simply. This is good for your faith but also helpful in case you have the opportunity to explain it to someone else. Here are some suggestions on how to do it.

1. Memorize some verses that explain the gospel. Here are two examples:

   1 **Romans 3:23 → 5:8 → 6:23** (This has been called The "Roman Road").

   2 **1 Peter 1:18 → 2:24 → 3:18**

2. Find some simple pamphlets that explain the gospel. Most Christian bookshops sell little pamphlets that explain the gospel in simple terms (and sometimes with pictures!). Have a look for some and learn how to use them.
3. It is a good idea to get into the habit of reading Christian books. Ask your pastor to recommend some books that will help you understand the gospel and to grow in your knowledge and faith!

Death and Resurrection of Jesus
The Crucifixion
Luke 23:32-49

He himself bore our sins in his body on the tree, so that we might die to sins and live for righteousness; by his wounds you have been healed. 1 Peter 2:24

let's get started

let's get started

Share Have you ever taken the blame for something you didn't do?

How do you feel when (or if) you are blamed for something you didn't do? (✔ Choose from the list below).

- ☐ Angry ☐ Revengeful ☐ Depressed
- ☐ Never happens (I have the face of an angel)
- ☐ Don't care ☐ Other? ____________________

Share your answers.

going deeper

going deeper

» **The crucifixion. Read Luke 23:32-39.**

+ What was Jesus asked to do three times in response to the insults given to him?

v. 35 "If he is the Christ of God, the chosen one, let him __________"

v. 37 "If you are the king of the Jews ______________________________"

v. 39 "Aren't you the Christ? ____________________________________"

+ Read the following verses. Who was Jesus interested in saving that day?

John 3:17
1 Timothy 1:15

+ We have seen earlier (Study 1 and 2) that Jesus knew what was going to happen to him. He willingly laid down his life and so fulfilled God's plan. Read the following two passages that spoke of Jesus' death 100s of years earlier:

Isaiah 53:3-10
Psalm 22:7-8, 12-18

+ Jesus knew his death would be a brutal experience. What does that say to you about him?

a criminal is saved... *Last week we saw that Jesus was substituted for Barabbas. In this story we see how Jesus also was the substitute for the criminal and how through faith the criminal received eternal life. Read Luke 23:39-43. What was the important difference between Barabbas and the criminal? (Hint: vv. 41-43)*

Jesus' death. Read Luke 23:44-49.

+ Jesus quotes a Psalm as he dies (v. 46). Look at Psalm 31:1-5. What does this tell you about what was going through Jesus' mind?

+ What were some of the incredible things the centurion saw and heard that made him conclude that Jesus was a righteous man (v. 46)?

v. 34 ______________________________

v. 38 ______________________________

vv. 42-43 ______________________________

v. 44 ______________________________

v. 46 ______________________________

The temple curtain temple is torn in two (v. 45). The curtain in the temple separated people from the Holy of Holies (the place where you could enter the presence of God - Hebrews 9:3). This area was restricted to the high priest and entry was allowed only once a year. However, the death of Jesus now gives access to the presence of God for all of us at any time. **Read Hebrews 10:19-22.**

FYI The sign of darkness...

One of the strange events that people witnessed at Jesus' crucifixion was darkness for about three hours. This w possibly a sign of God's judgment (se Amos 8:9-10). Look at the following verses that talk about the judgment God and the death of Jesus and wor out what the connection between t two is: Romans 4:25, 5:15-16, 6 8:1-2.

- How are we to view our relationship with God? (vv. 19-22)

- What can you say to someone who says:
  - "God feels far away"?
  - "I need a priest or a saint to speak to God for me"?
  - "I can't believe that God can forgive me for everything I have done in the past"

- How should our direct relationship with God influence the way we live? (vv. 23-25)

getting active

getting active

Helping each other

- How can we help each other when we doubt our relationship with God?

- In what ways can we "encourage each other as we see the Day approaching" (Hebrews 10:25)?

let's pray

- Thank Jesus for saving us instead of saving himself.
- Pray for people you know who have not yet turned to Jesus to be saved
- Ask God to help you to live out your faith as described in Hebrews 10:23-25.
- Share any other matters for prayer and then pray together.

Stay tuned Next week, we will look at the great news that Jesus arose from the grave!

For your eyes only:
The week ahead

For your eyes only:
The Week ahead

1. Personal Bible Reading

For the next couple of weeks, you will read the other accounts of Jesus' death and resurrection. These accounts vary from one another in detail as they were written from three other perspectives. The story, however, is the same and you will see many similarities to Luke's account.

My weekly Bible reading plan!

In the Gospel of Matthew, I read... (place a ✔ when you have read it.)

- ☐ Matthew 26:1-35
- ☐ Matthew 26:36-56
- ☐ Matthew 26:57-75
- ☐ Matthew 27:1-26
- ☐ Matthew 27:27-56
- ☐ Matthew 27:57-28:20

2. Memory Verse

Can you learn the memory verse at the top of this study (1 Peter 2:24)? Give it a try this week.

He himself bore our sins in his body on the tree, so that we might die to sins and live for righteousness; by his wounds you have been healed. 1 Peter 2:24

3. Prayer

Give thanks that Jesus died for you!
Pray for those who do not know Jesus.

Things that I can thank God for: ______________________________

____

Things that I need to pray for: ______________________________

____

Understanding forgiveness

The death of Jesus means that you can have forgiveness for everything you have ever done wrong… just like the thief on the cross. Jesus' death deals with our past, present and future sin.

Sin in the past: Many Christians feel guilty for past sins, even after they have asked Jesus to forgive them. Jesus' death is powerful and able to deal with everything we have done. Jesus not only took our sin, he also credits us with his righteousness (2 Corinthians 5:21). This is cause for great thanksgiving! If you are still struggling with guilt, here are some things you should do:

1. **Read** what the Bible says about grace (grace is receiving a gift we don't deserve). Here are some good places to start: Ephesians 2:1-10, Titus 3:3-7, 2 Timothy 1:8-10, Romans 8:31-34.
2. **Confess** your sin to someone you trust (1 John 1:8-9 and James 5:16). Often the open confession of our sin disarms its power over us. After you have confessed to someone ask him/her to pray for you that you can put away any guilt.
3. **Pray**: Instead of continually asking for forgiveness for a past sin, turn your prayer into thanksgiving for the assurance of forgiveness for that past sin.

Sin in the present: The correct response to forgiveness is to reject sin as a way of life (e.g. Romans 6:1-14, Colossians 3:1-6, Titus 2:11-12, 1 Peter 4:1-2). Rejection of sin is a sign that your relationship with Jesus has changed you. However, some Christians struggle with habitual sin. If this is you, here are some things you should do:

1. Remove yourself from whatever is tempting you (for example: if the sin is drunkenness, avoid going places where you will be tempted by alcohol. If the problem is internet porn then don't use a computer in a private location).
2. Once you have worked at removing yourself from temptation, ask a Christian friend or group of friends to keep you accountable for your actions.
3. Pray for help and forgiveness. This is a prayer God loves to answer! Also ask others to pray for you.

Sin in the future: The death of Jesus was a once-for-all sacrifice to pay for sin (Hebrews 9:24-28, 1 Peter 3:18). This means that Jesus had your sin in mind when he was dying on the cross. Faith in this once-for-all sacrifice gives us assurance of our salvation and certainty of eternal life (1 John 5:13).

The Resurrection

Luke 23:50~24:12

Praise be to the God and Father of our Lord Jesus Christ! In his great mercy he has given us new birth into a living hope through the resurrection of Jesus Christ from the dead. 1 Peter 1:3

let's get started

let's get started

1 Here are some opinions about what happens to someone after they die. Which ones do you think are the most popular with the people you know (choose up to 3)?

- ◯ Nothing
- ◯ Heaven for good people, Hell for bad people
- ◯ Heaven for everyone
- ◯ Heaven for followers of Jesus
- ◯ We are judged by God
- ◯ Hell for people who reject God
- ◯ Reincarnation (come back as another person or animal)

2 Why do you think many people are afraid of death?

The burial and resurrection of Jesus. **Read Luke 23:50-24:12.**

- What did they do with Jesus' body? (vv. 50-54)

- There have been many theories explaining why the resurrection did not happen. One theory is that the women went to the wrong tomb and found it empty. What are some clues that Luke gives us that discredit this theory?

Luke 23:55
Luke 24:12

- What was the message the two angels brought? (vv. 5-7)

- How did the women respond to the message? (vv. 8-9)

FYI Did you know.... the word "angel" in the original New Testament language means "messenger"?

- Did the disciples believe what Jesus had taught them earlier about the resurrection (Luke 9:22 and 24:7)? (vv. 10-11)

- Why do you think Peter ran to the tomb?

Why was the resurrection important?

- Have a look a the following verses and work our why the resurrection was necessary:

Acts 17:30-31 ____________________

Romans 1:1-4 ____________________

Romans 6:5 ____________________

1 Peter 1:3 ____________________

(See also 1 Corinthians 15:12-20. Here Paul gives the implications for us if Jesus had not risen from the dead.)

+ How does the resurrection give us confidence that Jesus has dealt with our sin?

+ How can the resurrection of Jesus help us when we fear death?

The resurrection and you.

+ An important question to answer is: "What happens to us when we die?" **Read the following passages.** What do they teach us about what will happen to us when we die?

1 Corinthians 15:50-53 ____________________

Colossians 3:3-4 ____________________

Hebrews 9:27____________________

getting active

getting active

Helping each other

+ What can you say to someone who thinks the resurrection is not important?

+ How can we help each other when we fear death?

let's pray

- Pray that we can have confidence in our relationship with God because of the death and resurrection of Jesus.
- Pray that we will not fear death because of our hope in Jesus.
- Pray that we will have the opportunity and the boldness to tell our friends about Jesus' death and resurrection.
- Share any other matters for prayer and then pray together.

stay tuned

Next week, we will learn about two people who met the resurrected Jesus.

For your eyes only:
The week ahead

For your eyes only:
The Week ahead

1. Personal Bible Reading

Last week, you read the account of Jesus' death and resurrection in Matthew. You will have learned more about what happened over that weekend that Luke did not cover. This week, you will read the death and resurrection account according to Mark. Mark is the shortest of the four gospels and so gives us a nice simple overview.

My weekly Bible reading plan!

In the Gospel of Mark, I read... (place a ✔ when you have read it.)

- ☐ Mark 14:1-31
- ☐ Mark 14:32-52
- ☐ Mark 14:53-15:15
- ☐ Mark 15:16-41
- ☐ Mark 15:42-16:20

Additional reading: 1 Corinthians 15 is a chapter devoted to the subject of the resurrection. Try to read the whole chapter this week.

2 Memory Verse

Can you learn the memory verse at the top of this study (1 Peter 1:3)? Give it a try this week!

Praise be to the God and Father of our Lord Jesus Christ! In his great mercy he has given us new birth into a living hope through the resurrection of Jesus Christ from the dead. 1 Peter 1:3

Give thanks for the resurrection of Jesus. Pray for forgiveness for things you have done wrong and are feeling guilty about. Ask God to help you know that your sins are forgiven because of the death and resurrection of Jesus.

Things that I can thank God for: ______________________________

____

Things that I need to pray for: ______________________________

Defense of the resurrection

The resurrection is crucial to the gospel message. Without it the Apostle Paul says our faith is futile and we are still in our sin (1 Corinthians 15:13-19). It is no surprise then that some people say the resurrection did not happen. It is important to engage with these kinds of accusations and learn what the Bible teaches so we can respond. Below are some examples of arguments against the resurrection. Look at the Bible passages and work out why these arguments are not valid.

argument 1: Jesus didn't die on the cross, but only fainted. After he was buried he revived, rolled the stone away and escaped.

Read: Matthew 27:62-66, Mark 15:42-45, Luke 23:46-49, John 19:31-35

argument 2: The Disciples removed the body over the weekend and made up the story about the resurrection.

Read: Matthew 27:62-66 and 28:11-15

- Describe the disciples before the resurrection: Matthew 26:69-75, Mark 14:50.

- Describe the disciples after the resurrection: Acts 4:13, 1 Peter 4:12-14.

argument 3: Jesus died on the cross. Someone else was mistaken Jesus. There are two forms of this theory: 1. Jesus died and someone else was mistaken for the resurrected Jesus. 2. Jesus didn't die, one of his followers did. When Jesus was seen later they assumed he was "resurrected".

Read: Matthew 28:1-10, Luke 24:13-31, Luke 24:36-43, John 20:13-16, John 20:24-29

Jesus appears on the road to Emmaus

Luke 24:13-35

For what I received I passed on to you as of first importance: that Christ died for sins accordin to the Scriptures, that he was buried, that he was raised on the third day according to th Scriptures, and that he appeared to Peter, and then to the Twelve. 1 Corinthians 15:3-

let's get started

let's get started

Share

Who is someone famous you would like to meet?

What is the closest you have come to seeing or meeting someone famous?

going deeper

going deeper

Jesus appears to two travelers. Read Luke 24:13-27.

- What did the two travelers believe about Jesus? (vv. 19-21)

- Why were they sad?

- What evidence did the two travelers have about Jesus' resurrection?

Verse 21 ______

Verses 22-23 ______

Verse 24 ______

- Why do you think the two travelers had trouble believing the resurrection of Jesus?

- What does Jesus say to them in response? (vv. 25-27)

FYI **Did YOU know...**

The expression "Moses and the prophets" is a way of referring to the whole of the Old Testament. Jesus was showing the two that the whole of the Old Testament was fulfilled in his death and resurrection.

Proof of the resurrection. **Read Luke 24:28-35.**

- What made the two travelers recognize Jesus? (v. 31. See also v. 16).

- What kind of proof do people often want in order to believe in Jesus? (Choose from the options below).

Seeing Jesus with their own eyes

Having Jesus speak to them

Having some kind of 'experience' of Jesus

Historical evidence

Other? ______

- Why do you think they rushed back to Jerusalem (seven miles in the dark) to see the disciples?

- The Emmaus story confirmed the witness of the women to the resurrection (Luke 24:1-8). Have you ever had someone tell you something that you did not believe until someone else confirmed it?

+ Why do you think people doubt the resurrection of Jesus today? (Choose from the list below and discuss your answers)

- ☐ It proves he is who he claims to be.
- ☐ It means he has to be taken seriously.
- ☐ Miracles are not possible.
- ☐ It means that other views about death are not true (e.g., reincarnation, non-existence etc)
- ☐ Other? ______________________________

+ What would you say to someone who doubts the resurrection of Jesus?

FYI not just a theory... The death and resurrection of Jesus is not just theory – it affects how we live today. Read: Romans 6:8-14 What does this passage say to someone who says..."It is okay to believe in Jesus and behave however I want"?

getting active

getting active

Helping each other

+ How does the story of Emmaus help us in our faith in the resurrection?

+ How can you help each other to live lives that reflect a true understanding that Jesus died and rose again?

let's pray

- Give thanks for the resurrection of Jesus!
- Pray for your friends or family who do not know Jesus. Pray that God will open their eyes (in the same way he opened the eyes of the two travelers in our study).
- Pray that what you have learned about Jesus in the past six studies will affect how you live.
- Share any other matters for prayer and then pray together.

stay tuned Next week, we will have another great Bible study!

For your eyes only:

The week ahead

For your eyes only:
The Week ahead

1. Personal Bible Reading

The first three gospels (Matthew, Mark and Luke) are called the "Synoptics" (which means they are similar to each other). This week you will read the death and resurrection story from the book of John. John contains some material not recorded in the other gospels so will give you even more information about the death and resurrection of Jesus.

My weekly Bible reading plan!

In the Gospel of John, I read... (place a ✔ when you have read it.)

- ☐ John 18:1-14
- ☐ John 18:15-40
- ☐ John 19:1-37
- ☐ John 19:38-20:18
- ☐ John 20:19-21:25

Also: find some time to read the passage not covered in the studies: Luke 24:36-53

2. Memory Verse

Can you learn the memory verse at the top of this study (1 Corinthians 15:3-5)? Give it a try this week!

For what I received I passed on to you as of first importance: that Christ died for sins according to the Scriptures, that he was buried, that he was raised on the third day according to the Scriptures, and that he appeared to Peter, and then to the Twelve. 1 Corinthians 15:3-5

3. Prayer

Thank God for the eyewitness accounts in Luke of the resurrection of Jesus. Pray that we can be witnesses to the good news of the resurrection of Jesus.

Things that I can thank God for: ______________________________

Things that I need to pray for: ______________________________

Our resurrection body. Many people wonder what we will be like in heaven. Will we be the same age as the day we die? Will we remember and recognize each other? Will we be telepathic? The Bible does not answer all our questions about what heaven will be like, however, it does give answers about what we need to know.

Some facts about our future resurrection experience based on 1 Corinthians 15:35-57:

1. **Our body in heaven will be different from our body on earth** (vv. 35-42). One is perishable (our earthly body) and one is imperishable (our heavenly body).
2. **Our body will be perfect.** Some words that describe the earthly body are: dishonor, weak and natural. Compare these with our heavenly body: glory, power and spiritual (vv. 43-44). In heaven we will have bodies that resemble the likeness of Jesus in the same way that on earth we resemble the likeness of Adam (v. 45-49).
3. **Our bodies will be changed in some way,** ready for life in heaven (vv. 50-52).
4. **Our heavenly body will be free from death** (vv. 53-57).

Jesus is described as the heavenly man (1 Corinthians 15:48-49) and his resurrection is a pattern for what will happen to us.

Some facts about Jesus' resurrection experience:

1. He had a physical body that could eat fish (Luke 24:41-43). However, his body was not like ours as he could appear and disappear (Luke 24:31, 36).
2. The disciples recognized him and could touch him (Luke 24:38-40).

Some other passages to read about the resurrection:
2 Corinthians 5:1-10; 1 Thessalonians 4:13-18; Revelation 21 and 22.

The impact of the gospel on our daily life. Jesus' death and resurrection are not merely historical facts but are the basis of everything we believe and do. This information affects our relationship with God and our each other. It also affects how we live in this world and the choices we make. It affects everything!

Make some decisions today:

1. Accept Jesus' death and resurrection by faith and give your life to the God who loves you.
2. Learn more about what it means to live the Christian life through reading the Bible regularly.
3. Meet regularly with other believers to encourage them in their faith and to be encouraged in yours.
4. Ask God to help you live a life that reflects the relationship you now have with him. When you stumble, ask for forgiveness.
5. Remember that Jesus died to pay for your sin. Commit yourself to rejecting the life the world offers you and live to please God.

ANSWERS TO QUIZ ON PAGE 6

- [x] Jesus died on a Friday
- [x] Jesus was crucified on a cross
- [x] Jesus was tortured
- [ ] Jesus had a fair trial
- [ ] Christmas celebrates his death
- [x] Jesus was betrayed
- [x] Jesus forgave the people who killed him
- [ ] Jesus came to teach us to be nice people
- [x] Jesus arose on a Sunday
- [ ] Jesus' body secretly disappeared

Other recommended resources for your youth ministry:

Small Group Bible Studies

Starting Out
By Ken Moser

Foundations for Christian Living
By Ken Moser

Work Rest Play
By Ken Moser

Big Issues For Today's Youth
By Ken Moser

Young Men
By Ken Moser

Young Women
By Julie Moser

Studies 2 Go
By Julie Moser

More Studies 2 Go
By Julie Moser

Luke: Who is Jesus?
By Ken Moser

Luke: Jesus' Parables
By Ken Moser

Luke: Carry Your Cross
By Ken Moser

Resources for Leaders

Programs 2 Go
By Ken Moser

Changing the World through Effective Youth Ministry
By Ken Moser

Creative Christian Ideas for Youth Groups
By Ken Moser

Youth Evangelism: Reaching Young People in a Way that Honours God
By Ken Moser

thank you

Thanks to Kathy Tyers for her proofreading editing. Thanks also to Sarah Smith for her work on the layout and graphics.